# The Blueprint

## 21 Days of Prayer

---

Itika Watkins

The Blueprint: 21 Days of Prayer
Copyright © 2021 by Itika Watkins

Cover Photo taken from Canva.com

All rights reserved. No part of this book may be reproduced or transmitted in any form or by any means without written permission from the author.

ISBN (978-0-578-92492-2)

## Dedication

This book is dedicated to the woman who feels like God has forgotten about her, life has dealt you a terrible hand, uncertain of what to do next and that needs a touch from God. If you are reading this book, take your time to actively pursue all that God has for you, especially this intimate appointed time with the God that created heaven and earth to speak to you clearly and freely.

## Table of Contents

Foreword ................................................................ 1
Preface .................................................................. 2
Introduction ........................................................... 6
Day 1: Wrestle until the Break of Day ...................... 8
Day 2: You Will Testify ........................................... 12
Day 3: The Process in Moving Forward ................. 15
Day 4: At the Root Is Trust ..................................... 17
Day 5: You Have No Reason to Fear ..................... 20
Day 6: Obedience .................................................. 23
Day 7: Help My Unbelief ......................................... 25
Day 8: Finding God's Grace ................................... 27
Day 9: God, Grant Me Access ................................ 29
Day 10: God, Give Us Strategy .............................. 31
Day 11: Life Is Spiritual: The Sacrifice of Praise ...... 33
Day 12: It's Time to Kill It ........................................ 35
Day 13: You Can't Have My Joy ............................. 37
Day 14: Help Us to Love ........................................ 39
Day 15: Monitor Your Relationships ....................... 41
Day 16: Unlearn It .................................................. 43
Day 17: Lord, Give Strength ................................... 45
Day 18: Healthy Mind ............................................. 47
Day 19: Waiting with Earnest Expectation .............. 49
Day 20: Ask and Then Pursue ................................ 51
Day 21: The God That Answers .............................. 53

Where Do We Go from Here? .............................. 55

## Foreword

When Itika initially reached out to me, she was battling with what God told her to do with respect to writing a book, which happens to me a lot in my arena.

Putting your heart on paper and sharing it with the world is not an easy thing to do and I had a front row seat for her struggles throughout this process.

I must say that I am proud of her for making it to this day…

She wanted to pen this book to help you get to what God has put in your head and heart to do.

Sharing her journey wasn't an easy one as she battled the doubts of whether her words would matter or not, whether what she had written was good enough—all the usual emotions aspiring authors feel.

And dare I say, she even walked away from her first project, but did so at God's request as He needed her to be in a posture of prayer!

This book is the result of her inner obedience coming to light during a time of turmoil in the world and within her heart and soul as well.

The Bible says that some things only come by prayer and fasting and that is indeed true!

May God bless and keep you as you commit the next 21 days to Him.

May you put all distractions aside and be fully in tune with Him.

May you get the answers that you need and be okay if that looks differently from what you envision.

Godspeed!

**Tammie T. Polk**
**Author, Speaker, Coach**

## Preface

This book came about after obeying God and going into a 21 Day Prayer Challenge, which started as secret Facebook group.

The Prayer Room was God-inspired. The women and men that were a part of this accountability group desired a deeper connection to God and to have higher accountability in prayer with other Believers. We sought God for one hour over 21 days for healing, power, and deliverance. We wanted a breakthrough in every area of our lives.

Those who were in the group were invited by a friend. I believe that friends pull you higher and closer to God. As a member of the group, each member was responsible for inviting others to prayer and being in prayer.

Our only explicit instruction for being in The Prayer Room was that it be a safe space to share our burdens that we are praying to God for.

What we discovered is that the season was changing for many of us and our response to the change in our seasons required **deliberate, intentional obedience.** Understand that you believe that your season is changing, like for many of us, your deliberate, intentional obedience will feel obscure.

*Unchained.*
*Unlocked.*
*Unleashed.*
*Unapproved.*
*Radical in nature...*

…but it is what is needed for you to get where God wants you to be.

This season is about running in pursuit of your Y-E-S.

Yes, to God's will.
Yes, to God's way.
Giving God, a surrendered yes for the remainder of your life.

***Don't ignore the promptings of God.***

***Don't ignore what you see.***

***Don't ignore what you smell.***

***Don't ignore what you feel.***

For whatever reason you are in prayer, I believe God will tap into every area of your life to make an impression in time for what He desires of you to say or do. You may have visions while you are awake and while you sleep. These unplanned, unusual things are necessary for you to obtain what God has for you in life.

***Don't ignore the scriptures that are spoken*** and their meaning for your life. God is ministering to His people through the power of His written Word.

If a breakthrough is what you truly desire, then you have decided, consciously, that God is ***BIGGER***.

***Bigger than your family issues.**
**Bigger than your marital issues.**
**Bigger than your wayward children.**
**Bigger than your horrible boss or the company you work for.**
**Bigger than your infirmities, ailments, and diseases.**
**Bigger than any issue that you can conjure up or think of.***

***GOD IS BIGGER!*** He is preparing to show you a mystery through the power of prayer.

This season is a one of offering great reverence and genuine praise. It will be your medicine. You will come to know and understand that God is not just **A** source but that He is **THE** Source.

God is going to deliver you from the demonic rule, forces, and generational curses that have had dominion over your life. Some of these instances may not even surface until you begin to turn your life over to prayer. You will discover what has been hidden and masked by things you have been involved in or people you hung around, but **NONE** of our hang-ups, schisms, and issues will be able to stand in your prayer room!

It is past time for the hidden things of your life to become exposed -- areas of unforgiveness, anger, rage, jealousy, anxiety, nervousness, covetousness, deceit, and mockery. Ungodly lusts, patterns, ways, and habits will be uncovered in Jesus' name.

***It's time to ask God for forgiveness.***

These things have been concealed and lodged in the shafts and grooves in your heart. You have buried these issues in your heart, locked them there, and threw away the key. Or, you have built a wall around your hearts, making it stony and impenetrable—not to hurt anyone, but to keep the pain out.

***There is greatness in your pain.***

Prayer will restore you, exposing the secret areas of your life and generational curses that may be making you physically sick.

The sickness may not be terminal.

It could be acne.

…or your hair falling out.

…or abnormal breakouts on the skin in unusual places.

***God will deliver you, even now.***

It is **TIME** to repent and ask God to forgive you for being unappreciative, unthankful, unloving, unreachable, inattentive, unapologetic, bitter, worrisome, easily bothered, easily offended, resistant to change, slothful, mean, contentious, and sluggish.

These effects *MUST* be dealt with!

***God is here to deliver us.***

Let's start this journey to prayer through the 21 Day Prayer Challenge. You can do this alone, but it would be so much better when done along with other blood-washed believers.

*<u>NOTE:</u>* This journal is only a guide. I hope that it is helpful in your endeavors to live a holy, separated, and prosperous life.

## Introduction

This challenge is meant to:
- unlock supernatural strategies to use in your life
- help you develop deeper intimacy with God
- help you get into alignment with what God has for your life, as you labor to do His will.

This challenge is a walk in humility, where you will begin to rely more heavily on the spirit of God rather than your ability, knowledge, or opinion of others.

Through prayer, you will unlock God's blessings, which will lead to you producing unimaginable results.

Often, we make prayer traditional, legalistic, and formal. **That is NOT what prayer is!** It is you taking off our shoes, washing your face, and sitting in front of a God Who already knows your thoughts, will, emotions, areas of lack, concerns, frailties, and infirmities. All that is **REALLY** missing is you asking Him to sincerely help you to do His will in the Earth.

**What is required of you during this time of prayer?**

The main task is to intentionally establish a secret place in your home or dwelling. Being intentional is more than *"finding the time"* but it is also preparing your heart and mind to receive God's answers, responses, and actions toward you and your requests.

It is also important that you have a blank journal that you can use during this time to write out your thoughts, feelings, and emotions that you experience throughout this time of prayer.

*Every feeling...*
*Every thought...*

*Every response...*

*... even what you may see visually, and smell are important during this time.*

I believe that God is going to affect every ounce of your body, senses, and emotions.

And I don't think they should be ignored.

These are indicators to either enhance or cause you to pray more about something for yourself.

## Day 1

### *Wrestle until the Break of Day*

### Wrestle /ˈresəl/ to take part in a fight.

### Scripture Focus:

"And he rose up that night, and took his two wives, and his two women servants, and his eleven sons, and passed over the ford Jabbok. And he took them, and sent them over the brook, and sent over that he had. And Jacob was left alone; and there wrestled a man with him until the breaking of the day. And when he saw that he prevailed not against him, he touched the hollow of his thigh; and the hollow of Jacob's thigh was out of joint, as he wrestled with him." (Genesis 32:22-25)

During this time that you have alone with God, you need to demonstrate your faith. Resist the urge to make excuses during this time. Identify the events going on in your life that are keeping you continually busy and, so much so, that you are missing out on the time that you have set aside to spend with God.

***Don't give yourself a way out.***

We do this when we do not want to face what we do not know of, what we don't understand, and even what we are afraid of.

***Let your faith prevail.***

Don't allow yourself to not spend time with God. Don't give yourself an excuse for neglecting this time.

As we wrestle with God, labor to leave no stone unturned.

Give everything over to God completely so that your effort spent in prayer will not be in vain.

Allow God to steal you away from your day, family, friends, and the busyness of life so that He can speak to you.

God wants to deal with every area of your life, even those dark parts. We cause ourselves to be distracted with life, so that we can avoid thinking about the trials happening to us in life, but God desires that you remove every distraction to spend time with Him.

In this hour, God is demanding your attention.

During this prayer time, God wants something from you.

God is ready to destroy your self-reliance.

God wants to be Lord over your life and everything in your life. For those of us who have been self-reliant and unusually independent, this will be a struggle for you. However, I promise that, if you surrender your understanding, you will begin to see your faith and pursuit work for your good.

***Stop worrying about how things will work.***

***Stop worrying about if things will happen as you planned.***

Release your control of when…and enjoy basking in the presence of God. Being in the presence of a Holy God is a beautiful thing. No longer will you wonder … *"When will it happen for me? …when this or that."* You will enjoy God, knowing that He has all things in His divine control.

God wants you to fully surrender your heart and mind to Him. It is so hard to pray with a full heart and mind. It is so hard to thank God and praise God for His mighty acts and wonderful works. He wants you to take this delicate, sensitive time to learn about Him more. This is not **YOUR** will.

***He wants the inner war to stop.***

***No more inner battles.***

***The battle over our minds.***

He wants us to **WIN**.
God will not make you ashamed. You will live.

God desires for us to get back to the basics.
Get back to your first love.
Regain your posture and attitude, which has been mired by life situations, people, and circumstances.

***Release every ounce of unforgiveness in this season.***

The favor of God is on your life.

You've been fighting for a long time.

Fighting your way through, in your own strength, has made you tired.

Your hands are tired.

Your mind is tired.

Your will has grown tired.

Your body is tired.

***Realize that we wrestle not against flesh and blood.*** (Ephesians 6:12). We wrestle against:

- Principalities, a hierarchy that rules and governs in defeat.
- powers,
- The rulers of the darkness of this world—a world that we are not of, but live in.
- Spiritual wickedness in high places.

You are tired because you have been fighting a long time and in y*our* physical strength.

To get where God desires your family to be, the deliverance that He has already given you, the wealth that is yours. and the best of health, you must put on the whole armor of God!

Why? "That we may be able to stand against the wiles (the deviousness, the stratagems that are employed of the devil and all other governing principalities) of the devil." (Ephesians 6:11).

The whole armor is required to withstand the evil day ahead (Ephesians 6:13) and we need prayer for the mind, will, heart and emotions.

### Building Your Blueprint:

- **What are you wrestling with that God is trying to take from you?**
- **Journal Prompt:** Quiet reflection allows you to hear in the Spirit what God is trying to get through to your Spirit (wo)man. If you cannot hear, write down the thoughts that you are rejecting and refusing to hear.
- **What scripture do you believe applies to your situation right now?**
- **Set your intentions in this prayer. What do you need God to do?**

# Day 2

## *You Will Testify!*

**Shame /SHām/ the painful (what we are affected by) feeling (the emotion or reaction that is evoked by the thought) of humiliation (embarrassment, disgrace, dishonor, discredit, disesteem) or distress caused by the consciousness of wrong or foolish behavior.**

---

**Scripture Focus:**
"And one of them, when he saw that he was healed, turned back, and with a loud voice glorified God, And fell down on [his] face at his feet, giving him thanks: and he was a Samaritan." (Luke 17:15-16 KJV)

---

Before now, I would have never testified of what the Lord helped me through. Each of us has a testimony of God's mercy, love, and grace.

Testimonies of what did not happen because we lived a directed and careful life, never straying from the beaten path…

Testimonies of the things we strayed away to, only for them to lead to us getting heaps of devil-ridden trouble…

***God was in it all.***

No matter the story, your journey to salvation was nothing short of a miracle. You may not think so right now but, by the end of the challenge, you absolutely will. Consider the price that was paid as ransom for you as a testimony and one you will want to share. Sharing our testimony is for others that they might be made free by the power of God, but what often hinders us is the shame we experienced.

***This is where the journey begins.***

***We are ridding our lives of the shame and the heavy weight we feel in telling our story.***

You want to be sure that you are delivered from what and who hurt you! This is vital to someone who is looking to be able to get through hearing your story and being delivered, healed, and set free.

The problem with shame is that you may not know how to pinpoint exactly what about your story is affecting you. Oftentimes, it happens through triggers. I'm not a therapist by any stretch of the imagination; however, I can assure you that, after going to revival after revival, and sitting with my own emotions then pursuing God in prayer, confronting the shame of your life's mistakes and failures can only be done through prayer.

***We are ridding our life of the shame in telling our story.*** There are so many beautiful things that will happen because of doing so:

- You will not be bound (John 8:36)
- You will feel 1,000 pounds lighter (Hebrews 12:1)
- You will open yourself up to attract other believers, opportunities, groups, and relationships (Luke 6:38)
- God will be glorified (Isaiah 60:21)

## Building Your Blueprint

- **What's on your altar? And why?**
- **Journal Prompt:** Quiet reflection allows you to hear in the Spirit what God is trying to get through to your Spirit (wo)man. If you cannot hear, write down the thoughts that you are rejecting and refusing to hear.
- **What scripture do you believe applies to your situation right now?**
- **Set your intentions in this prayer. What do you need God to do?**

# Day 3

## *The Process in Moving Forward*

**Forward /ˈfôrwərd/ onward so as to make progress; toward a successful conclusion**.

---

**Scripture Focus:**
"But his wife looked back from behind him, and she became a pillar of salt." Genesis 19:26 (KJV)

---

*The most dangerous thing to do when praying to God is to give in to the temptation to return to the things we left at the altar.* I'm not sure why we do this, but we all have done it some time in our lives and our walk with Christ.

*We return to the things that we left at the altar because we are used to them.* We have sat in our issues for so long that they have attached themselves to us or they define us.

*There is grave danger in looking back.*

We define ourselves as the woman who:
- had a child out of wedlock,
- got divorced at a young age,

- who never married,
- who failed high school and didn't get her GED

Although these things may have happened to us, they do not have to define us!

***We've become accustomed to being associated with our issues, infirmities, ailments, and problems***. Depending on how long it has been an issue for us, we may have even grown up with it. It also could have been caused by ***how we allow*** people to define us.

### Building Your Blueprint

- **Journal Prompt:** Quiet reflection allows you to hear in the Spirit what God is trying to get through to your Spirit (wo)man. If you cannot hear, write down the thoughts that you are rejecting and refusing to hear.
- **What scripture do you believe applies to your situation right now?**
- **Set your intentions in this prayer. What do you need God to do?**

# Day 4

*At the root is trust!*

**Trust /trəst/ is the firm [unyielding, unwavering, solid,] belief [faith, confidence, reliance] in the reliability, truth, ability, or strength of someone or something.**

---

### Scripture Focus:

"Trust in the LORD with all thine heart; and lean not unto thine own understanding. In all thy ways acknowledge him, and he shall direct thy paths."
Proverbs 3:5-6 (KJV)

---

Another reason we return to the things that we left at the altar is that *we don't truly trust God and believe that He is going to deliver us*. Why? We are not being delivered, healed, or set free fast enough, but that's because we are expecting answers according to our own programmed timeline.

If after praying to a true and living God you continue to return to your issue, you are battling with an issue of trust!

Your confidence in God's ability to deliver you from the feeling of the emotions, pains, and hurt is likely at an all-time low. It's even easier to believe that God will deliver someone that we know, or even a stranger, instead of helping, healing, or delivering us.

If you're not trusting God in any one area of your life, you're not trusting God in all areas of your life.

***We want our lives to be yielded to Him.***

***We want to stop arguing with God in our spiritual posture.***

***We want to accept His will for our lives.***

Depending on what the issue, hang up or problem is that you are believing God to bring deliverance to you for, you have got change your posture from a prideful stance; one that says, "I can take care of myself in this area". You've made yourself a little god and this is where you must repent.

***We want to be completely submitted to God's will and way.***

***We want to completely give up the struggle*** and fight in our lives where we are trying to protect ourselves from something that has not worked up until this point—you are in need of prayer.

## **Building Your Blueprint**

- **If you're honest, would you say that you've released 'everything' to God? If not, write down all your burdens and the reasons why you haven't given them over completely.**
- **Journal Prompt:** Quiet reflection allows you to hear in the Spirit what God is trying to get through to your Spirit (wo)man. If you cannot hear, write down the thoughts that you are rejecting and refusing to hear.
- **What scripture do you believe applies to your situation right now?**
- **Set your intentions in this prayer. What do you need God to do?**

# Day 5

*You have no reason to fear.*

**Fear /ˈfir/ an unpleasant emotion caused by the belief that someone or something is dangerous, likely to cause pain or a threat.**

---

### Scripture Focus:

"Ye shall not fear them: for the LORD your God he shall fight for you." Deuteronomy 3:22 (KJV)

"And the LORD commanded us to do all these statutes, to fear the LORD our God, for our good always, that he might preserve us alive, as [it is] at this day." Deuteronomy 6:24 (KJV)

---

There are thoughts of things that we have taken on which should not be the thoughts of a believer. *Fear is probably one thing that believers worldwide have in common.*

Fear of being hurt.
Fear of being lied to.
Fear of trusting someone.

We don't want to make a mistake in singing, writing, giving, loving, meeting new people, doing new things, and going to new places because we dwell in a perpetual state of fear.

***Fear torments and confuses the mind***. It causes you to be easily offended, intimidated, scary, doubtful, weary, weak, etc. Walking in fear causes a believer to have blurred vision, which isn't the natural state of a believer.

The more that we seek God, the more that God will come in and cause fear to leave. We must know that perfect love casteth out all fear.

We can risk loving somebody, even if we don't know if they'll hurt us. Why? God risked His son, Jesus, for us.

***Let's learn how to do new things, trusting in God.***

***Let's grow in the things that we are learning, trusting in God.***

***Let's experience new things, believing in God.***

***Let's laugh more, trusting in God.***

***Let us not shrink or draw back from the unknown.***

If we keep praying as a continual posture, God will deliver us from the torment of fear.

## Building Your Blueprint

- **What is the root cause of your fear?**
- **Journal Prompt:** Quiet reflection allows you to hear in the Spirit what God is trying to get through to your Spirit (wo)man. If you cannot hear, write down the thoughts that you are rejecting and refusing to hear.
- **What scripture do you believe applies to your situation right now?**
- **Set your intentions in this prayer. What do you need God to do?**

## Day 6

Obedience /əˈbēdēəns, ōˈbēdēəns/ compliance with an order, request, or law or submission to another's authority.

### Scripture Focus:

"And when ye spread forth your hands, I will hide mine eyes from you: yea, when ye make many prayers, I will not hear: your hands are full of blood. Wash you, make you clean; put away the evil of your doings from before mine eyes; cease to do evil; Learn to do well; seek judgment, relieve the oppressed, judge the fatherless, plead for the widow. Come now, and let us reason together, saith the Lord: though your sins be as scarlet, they shall be as white as snow; though they be red like crimson, they shall be as wool. If ye be willing and obedient, ye shall eat the good of the land: But if ye refuse and rebel, ye shall be devoured with the sword: for the mouth of the Lord hath spoken it." (Isaiah 1:15-20)

*Acknowledging disobedience has become popular*. We say things like, *"I am waiting on a word of confirmation"*. This is disobedience! We excuse away our own disobedience with reasons and justifications, which is likened to rebelliousness.

*There is only one requirement for obedience and that is willingness*. We must have readiness in our spirit and be prepared to be instructed by God at a moment's notice.

## Building Your Blueprint

- **What area of your life do you need more obedience in?**
- **Journal Prompt:** Quiet reflection allows you to hear in the Spirit what God is trying to get through to your Spirit (wo)man. If you cannot hear, write down the thoughts that you are rejecting and refusing to hear.
- **What scripture do you believe applies to your situation right now?**
- **Set your intentions in this prayer. What do you need God to do?**

## Day 7

*Help my unbelief!*

**be·lief /bəˈlēf/ an acceptance that a statement is true or that something exists. trust, faith, or confidence in someone or something.**

---

### Scripture Focus:
---

"And Abram [was] very rich in cattle, in silver, and in gold." Genesis 13:2 (KJV)

"And the land was not able to bear them, that they might dwell together: for their substance was great, so that they could not dwell together." Genesis 13:6 (KJV)

"Abram dwelled in the land of Canaan, and Lot dwelled in the cities of the plain, and pitched [his] tent toward Sodom." Genesis 13:12 (KJV)

"And Abram said, Lord GOD, what wilt thou give me, seeing I go childless, and the steward of my house [is] this Eliezer of Damascus?" Genesis 15:2 (KJV)

"Therefore Sarah laughed within herself, saying, After I am waxed old shall I have pleasure, my lord being old also? And the LORD said unto Abraham, Wherefore did Sarah laugh, saying, Shall I of a surety bear a child, which am old?" Genesis 18:12-13 (KJV)

"Then Sarah denied, saying, I laughed not; for she was afraid. And he said, Nay; but thou didst laugh." Genesis 18:15 (KJV)

"And straightway the father of the child cried out, and said with tears, Lord, I believe; help thou mine unbelief." Mark 9:24 (KJV)

Romans 3:3-4 (KJV) For what if some did not believe? shall their unbelief make the faith of God without effect? God forbid: yea, let God be true, but every man a liar; as it is written, That thou mightest be justified in thy sayings, and mightest overcome when thou art judged.

Believing and unbelieving at the same time is impossible! Believers can find themselves going away from believing in and following God fully. This keeps us in a perpetual state of double mindedness.

We've got to start seeing our situations, and circumstances the way God sees things, which we will not— unless we pray.

Also, being accountable in prayer with other believers is vital when you find yourself in this state.

### Building Your Blueprint

- **What has God told you that you're laughing about?**
- **Journal Prompt:** Quiet reflection allows you to hear in the Spirit what God is trying to get through to your Spirit (wo)man. If you cannot hear, write down the thoughts that you are rejecting and refusing to hear.
- **What scripture do you believe applies to your situation right now?**
- **Set your intentions in this prayer. What do you need God to do?**

## Day 8

*Finding God's Grace*

**Grace /grās/ the free and unmerited favor of God, as manifested in the salvation of sinners and the bestowal of blessings.**

---

### Scripture Focus:

"But Noah found grace in the eyes of the Lord."
(Genesis 6:8)

---

***Grace is part of the blessings that God give us.*** We ask God for grace in battles we are entering, but we must also carry the grace of God.

To carry any mantle, we need God's grace.

*The grace to minister.*

*The grace to evangelize.*

*The grace to be a ladder.*

*The grace for divine healing.*

*The grace to pioneer, to be a godly mother or father, to hold people's secrets, or to build a multi-million-dollar business.*

God is setting the captives free, creating divine connections, and healing people from all manner of ailments and diseases even during a pandemic.

God is making a way out of no way for those of us who are the first, and maybe only, in our families to get saved, marry, graduate college, and open a business.

## Building Your Blueprint

- **What do you need God's grace in?**
- **Journal Prompt:** Quiet reflection allows you to hear in the Spirit what God is trying to get through to your Spirit (wo)man. If you cannot hear, write down the thoughts that you are rejecting and refusing to hear.
- **What scripture do you believe applies to your situation right now?**
- **Set your intentions in this prayer. What do you need God to do?**

# Day 9

*God grant me access.*

**access /ˈakˌses/ a means of approaching or entering a place.**

---

### Scripture Focus:

"By whom also we have access by faith into this grace wherein we stand, and rejoice in hope of the glory of God." (Romans 5:2)

"For through him we both have access by one Spirit unto the Father." (Ephesians 2:18)

"In whom we have boldness and access with confidence by the faith of him." (Ephesians 3:12)

---

None of us know God's full plan for our lives, but we know that there is a divine plan for it, as it was for Jesus Christ.

As you go through prayer and become more obedient to His will and way, God is going to begin to unveil and disclose what He intends for your life.

How we approach God in this season is paramount to accessing what He has for our lives.

***God responds to our faith.***

Remember, without faith, it is impossible to please God. Faith in God gives us access. Our confidence in God and His ability to work in our lives grants us the access we desire.

## Building Your Blueprint

- **What makes you feel like you don't have access?**
- **Journal Prompt:** Quiet reflection allows you to hear in the Spirit what God is trying to get through to your Spirit (wo)man. If you cannot hear, write down the thoughts that you are rejecting and refusing to hear.
- **What scripture do you believe applies to your situation right now?**
- **Set your intentions in this prayer. What do you need God to do?**

# Day 10

## *God, give us strategy!*

**Strategy /ˈstradəjē/ a plan of action or policy designed to achieve a major or overall aim.**

### Scripture Focus:

"And the Lord spake unto Moses in the wilderness of Sinai, in the tabernacle of the congregation, on the first day of the second month, in the second year after they were come out of the land of Egypt, saying, Take ye the sum of all the congregation of the children of Israel, after their families, by the house of their fathers, with the number of their names, every male by their polls; From twenty years old and upward, all that are able to go forth to war in Israel: thou and Aaron shall number them by their armies. And with you there shall be a man of every tribe; every one head of the house of his fathers. And these are the names of the men that shall stand with you." (Numbers 1:1-5)

*We need a strategy in every area of life.* It does not matter how small or big it is.

We need God to have the right conversations, know the right people, learn new ways and processes, learn new cultures, open a business, go to school—it all needs a divine strategy.

We are returning to school after being out of for more than 20 years.

We are learning new devices and technologies. We are being brought into unfamiliar situation and circumstances, where we need God's divine strategic tactics to advance us. Failing to seek God for strategy only thwarts our movement when God gives us what to do naturally.

## Building Your Blueprint

- **Are you hearing the strategy that God is giving you for your life?**
- **Journal Prompt:** Quiet reflection allows you to hear in the Spirit what God is trying to get through to your Spirit (wo)man. If you cannot hear, write down the thoughts that you are rejecting and refusing to hear.
- **What scripture do you believe applies to your situation right now?**
- **Set your intentions in this prayer. What do you need God to do?**

# Day 11

## *Life is Spiritual: The Sacrifice of Praise*

---

### Scripture Focus:

[[A Psalm of praise.]] Make a joyful noise unto the LORD, all ye lands. Serve the LORD with gladness: come before his presence with singing. Know ye that the LORD he [is] God: [it is] he [that] hath made us, and not we ourselves; [we are] his people, and the sheep of his pasture. Enter into his gates with thanksgiving, [and] into his courts with praise: be thankful unto him, [and] bless his name. For the LORD [is] good; his mercy [is] everlasting; and his truth [endureth] to all generations. (Psalm 100:1-5)

---

**Praise is common among the upright.**

If we thought of praise as a weapon, we would never let the devil intercept our joy, block our breakthrough, or saddle us with depression.

The devil knows enough about praise to know that, if he can stop your praise by binding you with depression, sorrow, agony, pain, and hurt, you will not get the breakthrough that you desire.

When our minds are occupied and controlled by what the devil puts in our path, these things keep us from entering a place where we can praise God.

It keeps us from being able to set an atmosphere that is conducive to the presence of God.

### Building Your Blueprint

- **What is stopping your praise?**
- **Journal Prompt:** Quiet reflection allows you to hear in the Spirit what God is trying to get through to your Spirit (wo)man. If you cannot hear, write down the thoughts that you are rejecting and refusing to hear.
- **What scripture do you believe applies to your situation right now?**
- **Set your intentions in this prayer. What do you need God to do?**

# Day 12

## *It's time to kill it.*

**Kill /kil/ put an end to or cause the failure or defeat of (something).**

---

### Scripture Focus:

"For though we walk in the flesh, we do not war after the flesh: (For the weapons of our warfare [are] not carnal, but mighty through God to the pulling down of strong holds;) Casting down imaginations, and every high thing that exalteth itself against the knowledge of God, and bringing into captivity every thought to the obedience of Christ." (2 Corinthians 10:3-5)

---

While we can conquer the residue of things that have happened in our lives, there will be other aspects of our life that we will have to kill. You'll find that, the more you pursue God's will for your life, the more life interferences will begin to happen and more often.

*The goal is to get you off course, out of sync, out of touch with God's plan for your life.*

We have to use God's craftily designed weapons in our lives so that we can champion the life He has given us.

Prayer is often dismissed, but with the aid of prayer, which gives us unfettered access to a holy God, we will be equipped to defeat the wicked one.

### Building Your Blueprint:
- **What is lingering in your life, that you need to kill?**
- **Journal Prompt:** Quiet reflection allows you to hear in the Spirit what God is trying to get through to your Spirit (wo)man. If you cannot hear, write down the thoughts that you are rejecting and refusing to hear.
- **What scripture do you believe applies to your situation right now?**
- **Set your intentions in this prayer. What do you need God to do?**

# Day 13

*You can't have my Joy!*

**Joy /joi/ a feeling of great pleasure and happiness.**

---

### <u>Scripture Focus:</u>

"Then he said unto them, Go your way, eat the fat, and drink the sweet, and send portions unto them for whom nothing is prepared: for [this] day [is] holy unto our Lord: neither be ye sorry; for the joy of the LORD is your strength." (Nehemiah 8:10)

---

*You are in a fight for your life and to maintain your joy.* When situations get difficult, it is not uncommon for your joy to be the first thing to leave you.

But remember, no matter how hard or grueling your day may be due to the situations or people in your life, you have got to maintain your place of joy.

***This joy is rooted in your reliance on the Lord.***

That dependence and trust in God allows you to continue to be free in your mind, move as you wish, live as normal, and function as normal because God has your life under control. This is what the joy of the Lord does for us.

It allows us to not only move about life without worry or stress, but to also extend that joy to someone that does not have the same hope we do.

## Building Your Blueprint

- **Where did you lose your joy?**
- **Journal Prompt:** Quiet reflection allows you to hear in the Spirit what God is trying to get through to your Spirit (wo)man. If you cannot hear, write down the thoughts that you are rejecting and refusing to hear.
- **What scripture do you believe applies to your situation right now?**
- **Set your intentions in this prayer. What do you need God to do?**

# Day 14

## *Help us to Love!*

---

### **Scripture Focus:**

"And above all things have fervent charity among yourselves: for charity shall cover the multitude of sins."
(I Peter 4:8)

---

Having passionate, intense love for everyone besides yourself is what is required of you.

***If you display vehement, sincere love for others, your love should conceal any wrong done to you.***

The cliché most people tout is, "You can love, but you can never forget". This is a falsehood. You should be able to love and the love that you have for others will cover any wrong that happened to you. You are not a superhuman, though, so it requires fervent prayer to love beyond people's faults.

God knows best! After all, He gave His Son for us and, while His Son was here with us, we beat Him beyond recognition and hung Him until He took His last breath on Calvary.

***We can forgive and love, forgive again and love again.***

## Building Your Blueprint

- **Who makes you feel as if you can forgive, but never forget?**

- **How are you pursuing the relationships in your life differently?**
- **Journal Prompt:** Quiet reflection allows you to hear in the Spirit what God is trying to get through to your Spirit (wo)man. If you cannot hear, write down the thoughts that you are rejecting and refusing to hear.
- **What scripture do you believe applies to your situation right now?**
- **Set your intentions in this prayer. What do you need God to do?**

## Day 15

*Monitor your relationships!*

**Relationships** /rəˈlāSH(ə)nˌSHip/ the way in which two or more concepts, objects, or people are connected, or the state of being connected

### Scripture Focus:

The Book of Ruth

As we go through life, we get hurt more by the people we love and allow into our small worlds.

***Be wise as a serpent, harmless as a dove.***

***Not everyone needs access to all levels in our lives.*** There needs to be some separation. For where you are going, this separation will become clear and will happen. God will give us wisdom in this manner.

In general relationships, love your neighbor as yourself. We should show the love of God to everyone.

Family relationships can be physical and spiritual because this is a stronger bond between people. We still need to show them the love of God.

Destiny relationships are divine, life-changing, and propel your future. When the love of God is not shown, we lose them.

## Building Your Blueprint

- **How are you pursuing the relationships in your life differently?**
- **Journal Prompt**: Quiet reflection allows you to hear in the Spirit what God is trying to get through to your Spirit (wo)man. If you cannot hear, write down the thoughts that you are rejecting and refusing to hear.
- **What scripture do you believe applies to your situation right now?**
- **Set your intentions in this prayer. What do you need God to do?**

## Day 16

### *Unlearn it!*

---

#### **Scripture Focus:**

"That ye put off concerning the former conversation the old man, which is corrupt according to the deceitful lusts; And be renewed in the spirit of your mind; And that ye put on the new man, which after God is created in righteousness and true holiness." (Ephesians 4:22-24)

---

*As you venture to seek God more, there are a lot of things, ideologies, ways, and habits you as a believer must unlearn.* Some of these things are learned as religious practices while others are practices within your own family.

This unlearning has nothing to do with being properly raised, but rather learning how to live out our new lives in the fear and admonition of God.

His ways are higher than our ways. More importantly, His ways often contradict even the best of teachings and upbringing. *God will take something that we consider foolish and create a teachable moment for those of us who are way too brilliant for our own good.* God is looking for a people who will follow Him without question.

He wants us to trust Him even if we do not have all the details, know all the players, understand the meaning behind it all, and any other quirky habit or thought we may have.

He wants us to forget all the things we are leaving behind and put on this new way of being. This new manner of approaching life, under the direction of the Holy Ghost, is a new way of doing life.

As we continue to adopt a new way of thinking and living, we will find ourselves in great conflict with our past. But we are a righteous people and true holiness is a better way to live out our lives.

### Building Your Blueprint

- **What do you need to unlearn?**
- **Journal Prompt:** Quiet reflection allows you to hear in the Spirit what God is trying to get through to your Spirit (wo)man. If you cannot hear, write down the thoughts that you are rejecting and refusing to hear.
- **What scripture do you believe applies to your situation right now?**
- **Set your intentions in this prayer. What do you need God to do?**

# Day 17

*Lord, give strength!*

**Strength /streNG(k)TH/** the state of being physically strong.

---

### **Scripture Focus:**

Joshua 14

---

*God is giving you strength!*

When you focus on the problems at hand, it is easy to lose sight of the fact that God is strengthening you.

*If it were not for God, where would you be right now today?* You would have lost your mind. It is God keeping you going.

*Keeping you in good health.*

*Keeping you in your right mind*, even though it might have felt as if you were losing it.

When you look back over your life, you will see that God has been with you in every situation throughout your life.

If you depend on God, you will be strengthened.

If you follow God unequivocally, God will strengthen you.

The strength that God gives will nourish you, pick you up, and cause you to know that He is with you through it all.

*Accept the strength of the Lord today.*

*Allow Him to bring you into the perfect place that He has for you.*

## Building Your Blueprint

- **What are you handling in your strength, that belongs to God?**
- **Journal Prompt:** Quiet reflection allows you to hear in the Spirit what God is trying to get through to your Spirit (wo)man. If you cannot hear, write down the thoughts that you are rejecting and refusing to hear.
- **What scripture do you believe applies to your situation right now?**
- **Set your intentions in this prayer. What do you need God to do?**

# Day 18

## *Healthy Mind*

### **Scripture Focus:**

"Thou wilt keep him in perfect peace, whose mind is stayed on thee: because he trusteth in thee." (Isaiah 26:3)

***A healthy mind is a mind that is stayed on God.***

It is too difficult and very tedious to keep our mind on everything we have going on in our personal lives. It is too much to bear, which is not our responsibility as believers.

***Our minds and thoughts will be complete and whole if we keep our minds on God.***

When we keep our minds on God rather than the issues of life, we are demonstrating to Him that we trust Him and Him alone.

Do not allow your independence nor the false sense of strength you feel to give you the notion that your human strength is better than the strength that God gives.

### Building Your Blueprint

- **What is disturbing your peace?**
- **Journal Prompt:** Quiet reflection allows you to hear in the Spirit what God is trying to get through to your Spirit (wo)man. If you cannot hear, write down the thoughts that you are rejecting and refusing to hear.
- **What scripture do you believe applies to your situation right now?**
- **Set your intentions in this prayer. What do you need God to do?**

# Day 19

## *Waiting with Earnest Expectation*

**Earnest /ˈərnəst/ resulting from or showing sincere and intense conviction.**

---

### Scripture Focus:

For I know that this shall turn to my salvation through your prayer, and the supply of the Spirit of Jesus Christ, According to my earnest expectation and my hope, that in nothing I shall be ashamed, but that with all boldness, as always, so now also Christ shall be magnified in my body, whether it be by life, or by death. For to me to live is Christ, and to die is gain. (Philippians 1:19-21)

---

***Just because God has not answered your prayer yet does not mean that He is not going to answer.*** While we pray and wait, we want to show God a posture of waiting with earnest expectation. We want to wait until every part of our being believes that God is going to answer our prayers. We must know beyond a shadow of a doubt that God is a prayer answering God.

Being diligent and consistent in our prayer life and know that our God is awesome, amazing, and ready to reward us.

***In this time of waiting, we must have all assurance that God is going to answer and do according to His divine will for our lives.***

Times and seasons are too us all. Whatever we are waiting for God to answer, we want an answer in His timing and according to the divine plan that He has for our lives.

Understanding that God will not make us embarrassed about praying unto Him, look to Him for divine wisdom and direction, and a materialized answer.

## Building Your Blueprint

- **What have you been praying and seeking God for, but it seems like there's no answer in sight? Have you prayed fervently for it?**
- **Journal Prompt:** Quiet reflection allows you to hear in the Spirit what God is trying to get through to your Spirit (wo)man. If you cannot hear, write down the thoughts that you are rejecting and refusing to hear.
- **What scripture do you believe applies to your situation right now?**
- **Set your intentions in this prayer. What do you need God to do?**

## Day 20

*Ask and then pursue!*

**Pursue /pərˈsoo/ follow (someone or something) in order to catch or attack them.**

---

### Scripture Focus:

"And David enquired at the Lord, saying, Shall I pursue after this troop? shall I overtake them? And he answered him, Pursue: for thou shalt surely overtake them, and without fail recover all." (I Samuel 30:8)

---

*One thing people do not do in today's Christian climate is talk candidly nor enough about their distresses in life.*

When we do, we realize that our experiences and bouts in life may have nearly killed us; but not only that, someone has overcome them. This is the power in a community. This is the power of testifying and sharing our experiences of God bringing us up and out of our horrible situations. But instead, many are depressed and the devil has worn us out, leaving us to believe that we have no one and that we are the only ones going through.

Lean in to your community. Stop allowing the devil to torment and torture you in your circumstance. It's safe to say that we will each have our moments of distress as long as we live. Our communities of Believers should be building us up. We should be gaining strength and empowered to pursue and to continue to pursue the things of God.

The thing we must remember in every situation and circumstance is that God is not responding to what we are going through; He has a purpose and plan for each one of our lives. Do not lose sight of the fact that we have a real enemy. His only job is to kill, steal and to destroy. This is probably the most powerful aspect of community that we are not by ourselves. However, when we are alone, the devil can torture us to believe that we are frail and weak.

Pursue all that God has for your life!

### **Building Your Blueprint**

- **What is keeping you from following what you have been desiring?**
- **Journal Prompt:** Quiet reflection allows you to hear in the Spirit what God is trying to get through to your Spirit (wo)man. If you cannot hear, write down the thoughts that you are rejecting and refusing to hear.
- **What scripture do you believe applies to your situation right now?**
- **Set your intentions in this prayer. What do you need God to do?**

# Day 21

## *The God that Answers!*

**Bondage /ˈbändij/ the state of being a slave.**

### Scripture Focus:

"Wherefore say unto the children of Israel, I am the Lord, and I will bring you out from under the burdens of the Egyptians, and I will rid you out of their bondage, and I will redeem you with a stretched out arm, and with great judgments: And I will take you to me for a people, and I will be to you a God: and ye shall know that I am the Lord your God, which bringeth you out from under the burdens of the Egyptians. And I will bring you in unto the land, concerning the which I did swear to give it to Abraham, to Isaac, and to Jacob; and I will give it you for an heritage: I am the Lord." (Exodus 6:6-8)

We have gone through 21 days of praying and, in some cases, fasting and consecrating ourselves to reach the throne of God. All for what? For God to answer you.

*We dismiss God's answers in many cases because we wanted a different answer.*

God is answering our prayers, every minute, every hour, every day.

God is relieving us and ridding our lives of bondage.

Some of these restraints are self-inflicted, our current state, and inherited.

Nevertheless, God is providing answers and freeing us from what is oppressing us.

God is making these deeds known to us to fulfill His long-standing promises in our lives.

## Building Your Blueprint

- **Reflecting back, what is the most recent request that God has answered?**
- **Journal Prompt:** Quiet reflection allows you to hear in the Spirit what God is trying to get through to your Spirit (wo)man. If you cannot hear, write down the thoughts that you are rejecting and refusing to hear.
- **What scripture do you believe applies to your situation right now?**
- **Set your intentions in this prayer. What do you need God to do?**

## Where do we go from here?

### *There is a Community here for you!*

As I mentioned in the Introduction, the women and men that are a part of this group desire a deeper connection to God and to have higher accountability in prayer.

Each cycle lasts 21 days and we seek God for healing, power, and deliverance and we want BREAKTHROUGH! You will be held accountable in prayer and are asked not to reveal or share anyone's prayer outside of The Prayer Room.

If you are new to prayer, it is common for people stop praying when they don't hear an answer, see or feel a change in their situation or circumstance. Prayer is a love language and relationship that takes nurturing, development and time. I encourage you, that whatever you do, to not ever stop praying. As a matter of fact, *go deeper*.

I hope that your 21 days spent with God has been as life changing for you, as it was for me and for the women and men in the group at the start. I am not sure what cycle of prayer we are in, at the time of reading this book, but I pray that you have definitely found community. We continued in our cycles because some of us were not released from the things, situations and circumstances we were in. Some of us enjoyed the peace of God, through the power of prayer. Others of us attached ourselves to a community of women and men that genuinely care and have concern for each other, enough to pray with and for them.

**If you believe that you did not get an answer to your prayer, you are not finished praying.**

You are invited to join the Prayer Room: Belief, Faith & Breakthrough Facebook Community. This group is divine and was artfully put together to help other Believers find a passion for prayer. The community is here to help you rekindle and get back into a right relationship with God.

We hope to see and hear you in the room; we are here for you! In the meantime, I'll be praying that you come in and experience, embrace, and be empowered by the presence of God.

www.ingramcontent.com/pod-product-compliance
Lightning Source LLC
Chambersburg PA
CBHW051710090426
42736CB00013B/2634